LADAKH

ISBN : 81-7436-160-X

Second impression 2004
© Roli & Janssen BV 2001
Published in India by Roli Books
in arrangement with Roli & Janssen BV
M-75, Greater Kailash-II Market
New Delhi 110 048, India.
Phone: ++91-11-29212271, 29210886; Fax: ++91-11-29217185
Email: roli@vsnl.com; Website: rolibooks.com

Text: Nina Rao

Photo Credits:
Azad: p 3
Charu Dutta: pp 8-9
Hashmat Singh: p 43, 61
Pallava Bagla: Back Cover, p 4, 5, 14, 20, 21, 26, 37(bottom), 38, 40-41, 45, 46,
47, 54, 55, 56,62, 69, 70, 71, 72-73, 78, 79
R.K. Gaur: Cover, p 27, 36(top), 42, 44, 57(bottom), 60, 64-65, 66-67,
68, 69(bottom), 74
Thomas L. Kelly: p 2, 6-7, 10-11, 12, 13, 15, 16, 17, 18-19, 23, 24, 25,
28-29, 30-31, 32-33, 34, 35, 39, 48, 50-51, 58-59, 76-77

Map: Jai Kumar Sharma

Printed and bound in Singapore

Cover: A Ladakhi male in typical headgear
Back Cover: A lama opens an ornate door at Lamayuru monastery
Page 2: The statue of Maitreya, the Buddha to come
Page 3: A young monk sits contemplatively before a doorway

LADAKH

Manali ■ Zanskar

TEXT

Nina Rao

Lustre Press
Roli Books

Contents

Facing page: Monks take out a procession in Leh
Right: A Leh resident in full, colourful attire
Pages 6-7: Panorama of Leh town and the Indus valley
Pages 8-9: Chemrey monastery twinkles in the twilight

Photoksar village presents a contrast of mud walls and green fields

I

Tradition and Trespass

The approach to Ladakh by air over the Rohtang Pass transforms one's image of the Himalaya. The layers of tortured and stratified rock are a reminder of the Indian sub-continent folding up against the heart of Asia, lifting rivers and lakes up to incredible heights. Yet the world's greatest mountain range seems astonishingly diminutive, clothed in uniform layers of smooth and creamy snow.

It is astounding that in this terrain, once known as the end of the habitable word, communities have managed not merely to survive, but to evolve a rich socio-economic and cultural history. Initial wonder gives way to awe, the harsh black rock-face — faces carved with snow, clouds and mountain mists deters any thought of conquest. The fact that we are to skim across the high ridges, almost at touching distance and make a sharp and sudden descent into the Leh valley heightens our sense of the dramatic.

We plunge directly into the once unknown world of the Ladakh plateau. Having arrived seems an achievement in itself. Even by air unpredictable weather conditions make it difficult to reach Ladakh. Until the late sixties only Indian Air Force planes carried travellers there, strapped to benches and equipped with parachutes.

Over the Zoji-la Pass, the flight throws into relief the grimness of the old trade route that crossed the plateau to meet the Shyok river where the summer trail linking Ladakh to Yarkand on the Silk Route was located. The main trade routes that crossed Central Asia had been laid across mountains and deserts, linking Sinkiang in western China with eastern Europe. It took three months for the Chang Thang nomads and the traders on the Silk Route to go from Leh to Lhasa.

Ladakh's population is composed of distinct ethnic groups, predominantly the Mons, Dards and the Tibetans. The Mons are a pastoral community from the south of the Himalaya who converted to Buddhism in the time of the emperor Kanishka. In most villages, they are carpenters and blacksmiths, though they are now mainly village musicians who chant the great epic of the Ladakhi, the Kesar Saga.

The Dards are peasants of Indo-European stock settled in Dras. The Dards and Mons must have bartered their farm produce for animal products with the Tibetan Chang-pas, the nomads of Chang Thang. From Ladakh to Yarkand and Turkestan, the intrepid merchants continued to cross-fertilise culture when along with their goods they transported customs and technology. The ties are apparent in the common dress and linguistic unity, food habits and pastimes. It is almost as if the world beyond the passes has survived because the south-west-north-east axis was designed by nature to isolate the mountain communities, yet foster in them a curiously cosmopolitan outlook.

The importance of these passes is clearly evident from the historical development of the area. Today, Ladakh is a melting-pot, an expression of the living tradition of central Tibetan Buddhism and Islam combined with the Dogra, Kashmiri and Sikh cultures.

Fleeing monks, antagonistic princes, adventurers all found a way into these impregnable valleys, just as the purist mountaineer still prefers to find his — on foot. The contemporary wayfarer, travelling by road through the mountains around hairpin bends, can only dimly imagine the harrowing odyssey of travellers in the past. Today, the distance from Srinagar to Leh can be covered by road in two days at a comfortable pace, once the Border Roads Organisation has cut through the walls of ice in mid-June. From the plains, the route over the Bra Lacha-la is well marked. It is the trail that the nomads from the Change Thang plateau followed to bring their Pashmina goats for the shawl-markers of the Punjab. Historically, military campaigns have also used the Zanskar-Bara Lacha – Chang Thang axis more frequently than the Zoji-la route. Now that the Bara Lacha-la route has been made less treacherous by the all-weather Upshi-Manali road built

Top: A statue of the Padmasambhava inside Lamayuru monastery
Facing page: A boy lama in playful reverence

by the military, it seems as if the discovery of Ladakh only awaited the reach of technology.

Enter the tourist

Ladakh has always haunted the traveller's imagination because of its sheer inaccessibility. Zealously guarded because of its strategic location, it was opened to tourism as recently as 1974. It is no longer the valuable Pashmina wool or the rice, salt and tea of the old trade system that draws the traveller, but the composite world of Ladakh – the fascinating fusion of ancient religions, history and stormy political events which were the result of the proselytizing role of Buddhism. Although Ladakh is now a part of Jammu and Kashmir, it retains its independent character. This is what makes Ladakh unique – not its resemblance to Tibet, with which it was once identified, but with which ties have now become tenuous.

The Ladakhis as a people are naïve and spontaneous, as yet not undermined by the outsider. Their environment which defeats all those who are alien to it endows them with the capacity to retain their sturdy identity. The lonely tiers of the Lamayuru monastery appear to symbolise this spirit of endurance as do the defiant apple-green rivers that flow undeterred through narrow valleys. And the dun-coloured plateau seems to have beaten back the snow-bound, sunless gullies to provide a haven to those for whom Ladakh is home.

Given Ladakh's strategic importance, it has benefited by the creation of a logistical infrastructure, but has yet to receive a push towards industrial development.

Urbanisation is getting under way, but the intrusion of modernity is limited. The old trade routes through the central plateau have been converted into roads that cut through the bronze and silver setting of the Karakoram, Ladakh and Zanskar ranges. The Border Roads Organisation and the large military establishment maintain the roads but peasants and traders still use century-old routes.

A community in change

In a natural environment, which is by turns a hostile arctic desert and an oasis, water becomes the life-giving force, fundamental to the needs of development now visible in Ladakh. The pre-Buddhist peasant and wandering minstrel who

Below: Pen in hand,
a bespectacled monk
makes his notes
Facing page: Taking
sunny lessons at
Thikse monastery

sang about the heroic vision of the Kesar Saga, would be amazed to see the changes that have been wrought into his world which was then still young and free of man's pressing need for more room and greater resources. Now the emerging pattern of emerald valleys attests to his impulse for expansion.

The economic structure of Ladakh, sustained by the monastic system and what has been termed the 'emporium trade', is being eroded by government-sponsored construction activity and agricultural improvement. The collective spirit and the community approach on which the monastic system was based still survive, but the living standards of the people haven't improved much.

Only since 1947, when Ladakh became a part of the Indian Union, have Ladakhi skills been used for its advancement. Educated young Ladakhis have not been lured away by the promise of a brighter future outside their homeland but have stayed behind and helped in its development.

A prime example is the Stakna hydroelectric project - a tribute to Ladakhi engineers who have adapted design and technology to meet the challenge of stringent local conditions. The dam catches the Indus just below Hemis at 3,450 metres, and has been operated even in freezing weather. In a region where forests are scarce and temperatures plummet to extreme lows, the advent of electricity has humanised the environment dramatically. Only a frequent visitor to Ladakh would be alive to the radical changes brought about by electricity to the work-style, architecture and social pattern of the electrified villages. Evenings in Leh can now be stretched beyond the 11 p.m. deadline when diesel generators used to shut off.

Today, outside influences are tampering with Ladakh's historically determined scheme as the land is subject to undreamed-of pressures. The transitory visitor is unaware of the impact of his presence but it is obtrusively visible in the extending tentacles of the road network, in the pollution emitted by increased traffic and in the demand for services which are not expressive of the Ladakhi way of life. Once again, it is the historical vulnerability of Ladakh's economic system that becomes apparent as the genius of the people is mobilised to benefit the outsider.

Literacy in Ladakh

12-year-old Stanzin Zangpo did not know what a train was. He could not recognise a cow or a buffalo. At school, during geography lessons, he could not understand what a plain was and what a sea was. He only identified the jagged peaks near Diskit en route to the Siachin Glacier. When 30 Ladakhi children were brought to Delhi and taken to the zoo, they ran away in fright on seeing an elephant. The children were taken to Qutb Minar to learn about heights; they had never written a letter and were taken to the post office. After the Gujarat earthquake, they were taught about the causes and effects of quakes. They were present for the Army Day and Republic Day Parades to inculcate in them a sense of belonging and identity with the rest of India. Overjoyed with their new experiences in Delhi, one of them thought that the most exciting profession was that of an engine driver — a career that gave one freedom to travel and see the wonders of the country.

Preceding pages 18-19: Green fields sustain the community in the shadow of the Ladakh range
Below: Stok Palace nestles in a verdant valley

2

Landscapes of Colour

Ladakh brings one face to face with primordial nature. Mountains assume fantastic forms, deeply caverned and castellated, recessed by jagged ridges that glint in the sun even though the sky above may be leaden. There is a sense of dramatic contrast here, and heightened colour; tints of yellow, gold and ochre are predominant, but brown and green hillocks, blue and black boulders intersperse the oatmeal sweet of the sandy plains and the central plateau. Hamlets with their barley fields break the pattern of the mountain wilderness. From a distance, it is difficult to distinguish a village fort from its rocky background; all seem part of a marvellous unity.

The rapid changes of terrain are astonishing, One moment you are in a 100-metre wide valley with a panoramic view of an ochre wasteland. In the next instant, you see alluvial fans rising towards the foot of the hills. You may find yourself hemmed in by granite walls sometimes narrowing to a fissure no more than three-metres wide, where the sun does not penetrate and the sky is not visible; the earth is arid and unforgiving, with not a tree in sight, nor a footprint to follow. Yet just a few kilometres away you could stumble upon a rich meadow with lush grass for the mules to munch, migratory wildfowl from Siberia on the lake shore, dogs herding the peacefully grazing sheep, yaks being milked and scruffy little children playing in this pastoral setting.

In the National Park region, the highest in the world, piercingly cold winds blow through the gaps in the mighty ridges, which are often etched sharply against a magnificent blue sky or, as often, obscured by mist. If you are lucky, you can spot the rare ibex (whose horns are believed to be good luck charms which frequently adorn flat roofs), or the snow pheasant with a neutral tint that merges with the rocky terrain.

More visible with its luxuriant fur is the martnot, a mountain rodent of clumsy gait, which moves surprisingly fast to escape into its burrow .

At every step the landscape gets wilder. Bare rock protects the earth from the burden of heavy snow and the fierce height of the sun. On a clear, well-lit day, the fast-melting snow increases the volume of water cascading down the gorge. The silence of the mountains is broken only by the sighing winds, the call of an unseen animal, the whistle of a bird and the sound of water which resembles a song of joy as it dances down from its icy heights.

From Nymeo, where the confluence of the Zanskar and the Indus can be seen in the distinct blue and green shades of the water, up to Phiyang, where the river divides into a number of channels, the hillsides and the river bed are lush with extensive cultivation.

As the Indus widens, trees begin to appear and the valley opens up. Broad meadows interspersed with irrigation channels are visible from the road. Tangible symbols of Buddhism appear as one approaches a village: Chortens (Tibetan stupas) and mane walls (stones engraved with prayers and invocations, invariably kept to the right of the traveller) start to dot the landscape.

Closer to Leh, the mountains hem you in again, until a sudden dip in the ridge ahead gives you your first view of the capital. Prayer flags strung together sweep upwards to the rocky eminence of Palace Hill crowned by the fort and temple of Namgyal Tsemo.

Flat-roofed, whitewashed houses reach up to the walls of Leh Palace. The road winds past lofty, gaily painted chortens. The poplar grove thins out. Nine storeys high, with a frontage extending 75 metres, it towers over a pile of mud houses, its walls sloping inwards as if shrinking from the touch of plebian huts below. Further up the road is the broad stretch of the Leh bazaar, the open market that awaits customers from Delhi and Srinagar. In bygone days, it was the kafila (caravan) from Persia or Yarkand that brought the market alive with the 'emporium trade'. When monsoon winds made Indian ports inaccessible, the rice of Persia travelled up the Ladakh route. Along with rice, other goods from thousands of kilometres away also made their appearance. Even today traces of the 'emporium

trade' are evident, and the Leh bazaar is a good place to buy Chinese soup bowls, shoes, exotic jewellery, metalware and *thangkas.*

Leh town is enclosed by a low wall, interspersed with towers, approachable through a labyrinth of lanes. Ladakhi dressmakers, general merchants, dealers in antiques and bric-a-brac are present at every corner.

The Ladakhi male's dress is much like a Tibetan coat, with colourful facings and a cummerbund. The women wear a beautiful styled dress gathered at the waist and lined with brocade. It is worn with coloured pajamas in addition to which modern Ladakhi women also sport the Punjabi *chunni,* a long scarf. The most popular women's hairstyle is an intricate design of slim plaits held together at the bottom with a simple string or a gorgeous silver clip.

On festive occasions, women wear a unique headdress, the *perak,* shaped like a cobra-hood from red felt onto which uncut turquoise stones are stitched in rows of three, eight or ten. Two curved flaps covered with lambswool extend outwards over the ears.

A goatskin stole is another regular feature of the village woman's attire, replaced with brocade by the affluent. It Is a becoming adornment to a dress that is graceful in its simplicity, besides performing a functional role too by preventing the dress from becoming soiled by back-loads. Silk and velvet *gondas* (hats) are also a part of women's toilette, adding the desired touch of' colour for daily wear as the *perak* is too heavy to be worn. Ladakhi women have always enjoyed wearing and displaying jewellery – silver necklaces, amulets and rings, and in the old days, they would not go about without a silver toothpick, tweezers and ear-cleaners as well.

With weather-beaten faces, merry smiles and hats at a jaunty angle on top of their elaborate coiffures, the market women make a lively, attractive group. Wherever you go, in Ladakh a beaming *'Julley!'* will greet you and soon it becomes quite spontaneous for you to call out *'Julley!'* yourself. Without your being aware of it, your identification with Ladakh is well on its way.

Oases and deserts

Climb any height around Leh and you cannot fail to notice the contrast of stony desert and luxuriant fields; patches of green

Facing page:
Traditional Ladakhi
shoes ornamented
with woollen strips
Below: A vegetable
vendor in Leh bazaar

25

A Princess's legacy

Legend has it that one of the Spiti princesses found Ladakh insufferably cold and frequently complained of earache. She was advised to cover her ears and so began the fashion of wearing sable earmuffs attached to the *perak*. Her original *perak* can be seen in the Stok Palace Museum. Though sable earmuffs, which used to come from Yarkand, are now rarely seen, the uncut *per* or turquoise is still smuggled in from China along with velvet for the Ladakhi robe, the *goncha*. A good *perak* is a treasured heirloom handed down from mother to daughter. It is a costly item and the just pride of the owner who vaunts its royal sweep from crown to waist.

enclosed by stone walls in the midst of which flat-roofed houses freshly white-washed, appear like lotus gardens. Sometimes the village hangs at the very edge of a cliff, sometimes it lies scattered across a valley. Below Leh, flows the Indus; the river has travelled a fraction of its 1,600-kilometre journey to the Arabian Sea, and is yet to reach its full potential. The water is pea-green and placid, except on bright and sunny days, when by mid-afternoon the rapidly melting snow adds sparkle to it. Then it is like a ribbon of colour.

The Indus region is a veritable garden where summer stretches from June to October, permitting double-cropping, and the autumn brings a harvest of fruit. In Chang Thang, the landscape allows for no cultivation and the nomad population is constantly on the move, herding its flocks of sheep and Pashmina goats in search of pastures. The length and severity of winter is responsible for the acute poverty of Dras. Although located on the Leh-Srinagar road, it seems to have been passed over by development. In Zanskar, a judicious mix of intensive cultivation and livestock breeding has overcome the problem of the long snow-bound winter. Willow plantations supplement the winter supply of fuel that comes to Ladakh at a high cost. Now Zanskar is a surplus area sending butter to Leh and grain to Chang Thang. The same

Facing page: The *perak*
Below: Ladakhi women dressed in traditional finery during a folk dance
Pages 28-29: Quiet flows the Indus — though history has seen people constantly at war along its banks

pattern of development is visible in Kargil, the Suru valley and Chigtan.

Wherever the land permits, agriculture is the main occupation. At lower heights, the main crop is wheat, an important ingredient of the Ladakhi bread – *tagi*. The other staple is *sattu*, 'naked' barley (a variety of barley that grows without a husk), which is considered the poor man's food, as the well-to-do Ladakhis have adapted to the Kashmiri custom of eating rice. Old tales describe at length banquets where rice was served as a delicacy, but today the availability of rice has made the pilaff commonplace. Along the course of the Indus, fruit cultivation is a common supplement to grain, and the principal fruit of Ladakh is the *khumani* (apricot). Delicious varieties of grape and melon also prosper in the intense summer.

Walking along the dry channels in the fruit garden, one is often surprised to find animals grazing unhindered in the fields. No one turns them away since animal dung is a valued source of fertiliser. In the town, human refuse is also carefully husbanded by the peasants who come at the start of winter with a cart-load of mud, which is then piled up in the traditional toilet, a dry closet raised a few feet above the ground. At the start of the spring sowing, the peasant families collect all available labour to clear out the soil mix and lay it over the fields. In this way, the peasant has his supply of manure, which has been adequately processed during the inhospitable winter, and at the same time, the town is cleaned.

In the Asiatic tradition, agricultural operations depend heavily on livestock and in this region too, every rural family will try to buy a *dzo* (a hybrid of a male yak and a cow) and several cows. In addition, every village has a *gon-yak*, the community stud, which is tilled upon to perform his only duty during the mating season.

Irrigation is by water from snow-fed systems led into the fields by an intricate system of channels, the direction of the flow being changed by blocking a channel with a clod of earth. It is generally accepted that women work in the fields, perhaps because the men were earlier needed as porters accompanying the caravans, when trade was the principal activity. After the sowing, the weeding process begins, with the weeds too augmenting another scarce commodity, fodder.

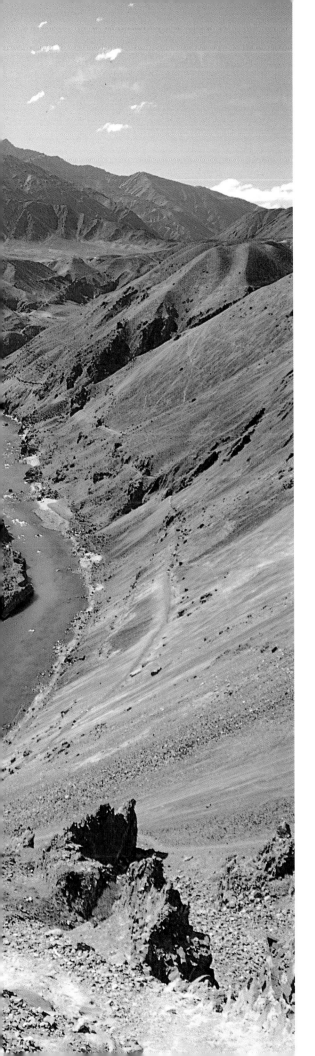

As the altitude increases, the peasant adapts his cropping patterns. He follows a culture that glorifies nature, militates against waste and is guided by the experience of its elders in keeping intact the organic protective system. Trees, animals and man adapt to an environment that is known to be benevolent to those who observe its laws.

Indus: River of bounty

Early Tibetans believed that the Indus rose in the holy lake of Mansarovar. However, expeditions place the source of the river north of the lake, but it does flow through the lake when it goes for a *parikrama* around (encircles) the holy mount Kailash, on its long journey to the sea. Known as the Sita, it passes through the Lion's mouth to change direction and turn north. Now, it is called the Sindhu. The warm waters of the Indus, once taken – it is said – could transform one into a lion. The history of conquest and war across the Indus would give credibility to the legend, yet the people of Leh are as gentle as lambs.

The Indus derives its name from the Sanskrit word, Sindhu. The Greeks called it the Sinthos, a name then used to represent those who lived beyond the river. The Rig Veda describes the medicinal plants to be found along its banks; some are a part of the *Amchi* medicinal system. The river has given its name to the Indus Valley civilisation and its heritage still informs our lives.

The Indus is now, the site of a new festival, Sindhu Darshan. This festival attempts to bring together all spiritual streams that have combined to create the spirit of being Indian. As priests, lamas and politicians converge on the banks of the river, traditional music and chanting begin. Once known as the Leh summer festival, the Sindhu Darshan includes cultural and sporting events but has moved to the bank of the river from the balcony of Leh Palace. This shift represents the transformation of Ladakh from an independent kingdom into a part of the Indian Union.

3

A Rugged History

Much of the early history of Ladakh is shrouded in legend, but there are rock inscriptions, chronicles, Chinese and Persian texts, as well as modern research, to support and authenticate it. Two dynasties, the Lha-Chen and the Namgyal, dominated the early and medieval period of Ladakhi history and were closely associated with protecting its independence, until the British in India attempted to bring Ladakh into their sphere of influence through their Dogra allies.

The political history of Ladakh as an independent kingdom is generally said to begin with the setting up of a Tibetan dynasty in AD 950. Prior to that, Ladakh must have shared in the fluctuating fortunes of an area that stretched from western Tibet to Kashmir in the south and Baltistan in the upper reaches of the Indus valley. Three ambitious neighbours, the kingdoms of Kashmir and Tibet and the empire of China, played a role in the early history of Ladakh. No authentic sources have been identified, but their involvement is clear.

From early Ladakhi history, we learn of Lang Darma, a central Tibetan ruler, who, resenting the concentration of secular and religious powers in the hands of the monks, began driving them out of the region. In AD 842, a monk assassinated him and his death is still celebrated at the Hemis festival with the dismembering of a *tsampa* doll, as the culmination of the first day's mystery play.

Ny-ma-gon, a descendant of Lang Darma, ruled an area to the east of modern Ladakh in the ninth century, but his sovereignty covered the area up to Zoji-la. He is said to be the father of the first independent Ladakhi dynasty. His eldest son, Pal-gyi-gon, was given the western area of the kingdom, and the middle son received Guge, the area south-west of Lake

The masked figures
in the Cham dance
enact the struggle
between good and evil

Mansarovar. His direct descendants formed the Lha-Chen dynasty that is said to have continued up to the fifteenth century, when the Namgyal kings, a minor branch of the Chens, established a new dynasty at Shey.

Western Ladakh was a loose federation of warring principalities, a weakness exploited first by the Kashgar kings and later by the Kashmiris. But in the reign of the Namgyals, despite the victory of Islam, the development of the monastery system continued to spread over the central plateau. Tashi Namgyal's monument in Leh stands as proof of his victory over the Islamic occupation. Jamyang Namgyal succeeded in bringing the Buddhist and Islamic forces together by his marriage to the Balti princess, Khatun, daughter of Ali Mir, the ruler of Skardu. Although according to legend, Jamyang is said to have converted to Islam to win the hand of the woman he loved, it was actually for harsher political compulsions.

Also, in an astute counter-balancing move, the Balti princess was proclaimed an incarnation of the White Tara, the Buddhist female deity. Thus, where once Balti armies had plundered and destroyed all the monasteries of central Ladakh, a period of stability and independence was ensured for the kingdom. The story goes that when Gyal Khatun was pregnant her father had a vision of a lion leaping into her womb; this apparently foretold the birth of the legendary Sengge (literally 'lion') Namgyal.

Even though the Lha-Chen dynasty was the inheritor and preserver of the Tibetan royal hours, it was the Namgyal dynasty that played the crucial role of Buddhism's protector. It faced the constant incursions of the Baltis and the Mughals in the west and Kashgar and Tibetan attacks from the east. Leh and Shey had been the citadels of Buddhism up to this point but after the Balti kingdom fell under Islamic influence, the centre of Buddhism shifted to Bagso and Tingmosgang. The plundering hordes now came in search of the fabulous wealth of the monasteries. The heartland of Ladakh was no longer safe. The Suru valley up to Kargil had already converted to this new and forceful religion, but under their rulers, the population of central Ladakh held firm. It is this success that gave them the epithet Namgya — 'Victorious', and the Namgyal deities on Namgyal Tsemo hill overlooking Leh are said to contain the bodies of the enemies of the dynasty, under the images of the Lords of the Four Seasons.

Militarily, Sengge Namgyal consolidated his kingdom by waging a successful campaign to subdue the kingdoms of Zanskar and Guje in the east. However, in a bid to restore the ravages of earlier Balti invasions he took on the combined Mughal and Balti armies in the west, and incurred a major defeat. In exchange for peace, the Mughals demanded a tribute to be paid to their governor in Kashmir.

Sengge Namgyal never actually paid the tribute. However, it was this defeat which provided the moral justification for Kashmir to subsequently lay claim to Ladakhi territory. On the religious front, Sengge Namgyal came under the influence of the monk, Stag-tsang-ras-chen, and there the king and the monk tried to rescue Buddhism from Islamic advances by establishing various monasteries at Hanle, Fiemis and Stakna as well as Chemre.

As had happened in many principalities where religion and state power are closely aligned, Delegs, the son of Sengge Namgyal, decided to embark on a military expedition that had more to do with religious solidarity than with the interests of Ladakh. Ill-advisedly, he intervened in a dispute between Tibet and Bhutan where the Red Hat order of monks was predominant. Tibet allied with the Mongols to attack Ladakh and Delegs had to appeal to the Mughals in Kashmir for help.

The condition imposed by the Mughal ruler was that Delegs would have to convert to Islam, build a mosque at Leh and ensure a monopoly of the raw Pashmina trade to Kashmir. But once the Mughal army withdrew, the Tibetans returned to subdue Delegs, and extracted a tribute in the form of the Lo-pchak mission.

The Tibetan influence did not stop at the Lo-pchak tribute, which interestingly was in the hands of leading Muslim traders who brought back not only items of trade from Tibet, but also several social customs: The *Gpa* administrative system based on a consensus of opinion among the village elders, the tradition of primogeniture and the induction of the younger son into the monastery. All these institutions ensured the survival of Buddhism under the spiritual leadership of the Dalai Lama – an influence that is recognised even today with the current Dalai Lama resident in India. However, as Muslims began to participate increasingly in trade and more Kashmiri traders began to settle in Ladakh, the Islamic influence also continued to grow.

The devil dancer
takes the floor and
regales the crowd

After the reign of Sengge, Leh grew in importance, replacing the ancient capital of Shey. It was also more conveniently situated on the approach route to Khardong-la, the main summer trail to Yarkand. The fact that a strategically placed capital was no longer of primary importance underlies the role that mercantilism was beginning to play in the economy of Ladakh. That a magnificent palace was built at Leh was an indication of the self confidence of Sengge and other Namgyal rulers who were, in fact, occupying an uncertain position between Buddhist Tibet and Muslim Kashmir. Although neither neighbour interfered in the internal affairs of Ladakh, its external relations were severely restricted.

A dynasty falls

The decline of the Namgyal dynasty began with the familiar and tragic emergence of family intrigues, succession disputes and rulers who were unfit, mentally and physically, to face the challenge of the Sikh-Dogra alliance in the south. Kashmir came under Sikh rule in 1819. Both Ranjit Singh and his powerful vassal, Gulab Singh of Jammu, saw the importance of the Pashmina trade which had been diverted by the British to their area of control, via Kinnaur. This had robbed the Kashmir shawl-maker of his source of raw material. To gain control over this lucrative trade, Gulab Singh opened the Kishtwar trail and planned to invade Ladakh, in Ranjit Singh's name.

William Moorcroft, an English army veterinary doctor, in the course of his travels from 1820-22, had pointed out to Tshe-Spal Namgyal the danger of Dogra ambitions. Neither the Ladakhi king nor the British government in India heeded Moorcroft's intelligence.

The Dogra army marched through Ladakhi territories via Zanskar and captured Leh. In the winter of 1841, Zorawar Singh, a general in Gulab Singh's army, extended the scope of the campaign to include central Tibet. The attraction was the mercantile centre of Gartok that was the source of the Pashmina trade. With the helpful freezing of the river in winter, the temptation to bring Gartok within the Dogra domain was irresistible and, of course, there was the added lure of the fabulous wealth of the Tibetan monasteries.

Pursuing his ambitions, Zorawar Singh conquered western Tibet up to Taklakot when he began to make a series of

strategic errors, as a consequence of which he found himself entrenched at a height of 4,500 metres in severe weather with supply lines to his base disrupted. Besides, Tibet was not facing him alone; the Chinese empire stood behind its Tibetan vassals. Though this was the last of the famous campaigns of a remarkable soldier, and the death of Zorawar Singh multiplied the difficulties confronting his forces, later Dogra successes put an end to the common belief that the conquest of Ladakh had been entirely due to him. The Dogra incursions ended Ladakh's status as an independent kingdom with the treaty of Leh in 1842. Tibet recognised the Dogras as the rulers of Ladakh and Jigmet Namgyal became a vassal king, subsequently known as the Jagirdar of Stok.

Top: The Hemis Thangka
unfurled once in 12 years
in the courtyard where
the festival is held
Facing page (below):
The Hemis monastery

Below: One of the
many drums that provide
the rhythm to the
Cham dancers
Facing page: A typical
Ladakhi kitchen, the
centre of family life

Even today, the royal family is resident in the Stok Palace, where tourists can visit the family museum and perhaps get a glimpse of the *Gyal-mo,* the queen. In the flux of Anglo-Sikh relations, which were guided by British interests in Punjab and beyond, the Dogras continued to administer the districts of Leh and Baltistan.

From this time, Ladakh was no longer allowed to remain a blank space on the map of the region. Members of British expeditions and explorers wrote about journeys to Ladakh in the late nineteenth century and the early twentieth century. As a consequence, the Jesuits set up their first mission in 1885, which introduced a new value system into the Buddhist citadel.

The Moravians, who established a permanent mission, have been credited with setting up the first allopathic dispensary and the First European school, without which the Western process of modernisation could not have been contemplated. Today, the modern professionals in Ladakh are descendants of those families who were converted in the first dynamic changes that took place in our times.

As British rule in India disintegrated, Ladakh too suffered the fate of Partition in 1947. With the accession of Kashmir to India, by the last Dogra king, Hari Singh, Pakistan went to war and captured a strategic position in the subcontinent.

This territory has been a source of constant friction between the two neighbours due to the military importance of the region. It was only in 1950 that the highlands of Sonamarg were linked with the Ladakh plateau by road, integrating it with India, while its age-old ties with arid Sinkiang remain severed. In 1962, the Nubra valley became a severed. In 1962, the Nubra valley became a permanent Army camp, reinforcing these links.

This makes Ladakh's socio-cultural institutions sensitive to encroachment, which follows from the changes taking place in the rest of the country. Ladakh is now a backward district of India – one of the largest – recently further sub-divided into the districts of Leh and Kargil. Gilgit has remained in Pakistan as a part of Occupied Kashmir and the Ladakhi people cut off from their history. But they jealously guard their identity, and neither Pakistan nor India has been able to assimilate them entirely.

The Lo-pchak mission

The Treaty of Tingmosgang sent a trade mission from Leh to Lhasa every three years. It carried gold, saffron and textiles as offerings to the Dalai Lama as well as gifts for other important Lamas. Apart from the ceremonial offerings, the Lo-pchak mission was allowed to carry 200 animal loads of trade goods for which the Tibetans provided free porterage. Thus it was a profitable enterprise and there was no constraint for non-Buddhists to run this mission. The Government of Jammu and Kashmir continued the mission and Muslim merchants managed it.

In return, a yearly trade mission came from Lhasa to Leh. It carried 200 animal loads of tea and was known as the Cha-pa caravan. Tea was carried in the form of bricks of compressed tea leaves that were easy to transport. This tea was used in the whole of Kashmir.

The mission carried back dried apricots. The travel time for the two missions was two-and-a-half months.

The route was through uninhabited country and the roads were under the control of brigands. The robbers, however, respected the religious cargo of the Lo-pchak and never attacked it. Private traders could lose their merchandise but the robbers always allowed them enough horses and mules stocked with essentials to survive the return journey.

Between 1940 and 1945, the two missions came to an end and India's trade with Tibet shifted to Kalimpong. A world-view was thus lost with the re-routing of trade between the two regions.

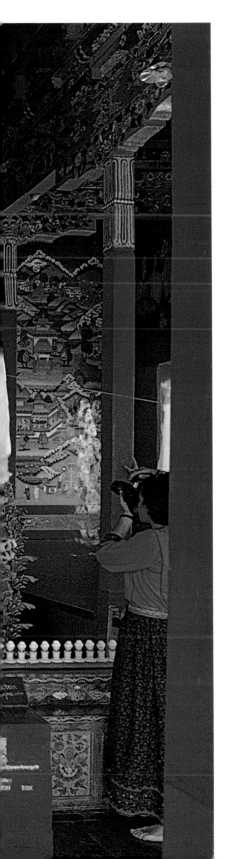

4

The Rituals of Religion

Politics and national interests have been inextricably and inevitably linked with religion in Ladakh. The success of Buddhism here was not simply a matter of vanquishing its adversaries outside Ladakh – Brahminism in India and the Bon Chos in Tibet. It was the unifying role it played in enlarging autonomous tribal clans into centralised feudal kingdoms. When fleeing monks and the laity met with strong resistance from local principalities, they were forced to assume a martial character, which ironically added a warlike dimension to a pacifist religion. Forts and monasteries grew apace as expansionist kingdoms consolidated their temporal and spiritual powers by extending their frontiers, so establishing Buddhism in Ladakh. Song-sen-gam-po, a legendary figure, was one such tribal chief, and in stories about him it is often difficult to sift fact from fiction. Yet it is true that he made deliberate use of' religion by contracting marriages with Buddhist princesses from Nepal and China to secure his position, and so founded the first Buddhist kingdom in Tibet. In strategy, he was an inspiration for later Ladakhi kings.

Ladakhi Buddhism is usually identified with Tibet, although the original inspiration came from Kashmir, probably during the Kushan period. It was later that the Tibetan branch established itself under what is termed the Second Advancement. This was Buddhism in its more developed and institutionalised form, inspired by the teachings of the Indian monks, Padmasambhava and Atisa. They had sought asylum in Tibet when Buddhism lost its royal patronage in India, and wanted to reflect the teachings of Sakyamuni as sincerely as possible.

Central to the Buddha's teaching was the belief that every soul has the capacity to reach a state of enlightenment

A representation of the
Avalokiteswara Buddha,
the compassionate one
who is endowed with 11
heads and a thousand
hands, at Alchi

without the assistance of priests or rituals. Nirvana could be achieved by following the reformist or middle path. Mahayana Buddhism adds a further condition to the Noble Path by demanding the virtue of compassion. Thus, no Boddhisattva can contemplate Nirvana selfishly while other souls are still bound to the wheel of mundane existence that is the source of their suffering.

The complexity of Buddhism lies in this concept, where the Bodhisattva returns to the world in several incarnations, striving for the liberation of mankind. A thousand Buddhas, of whom Sakyamuni is the fourth, will have to seek rebirth for the liberation of human souls. With the development of the Vajrayana school – the vehicle of the Thunderbolt – Tantric elements from Hinduism also merged into Buddhism. In particular, the feminine principle of power was introduced. As Buddhism spread, it did not suppress the well-developed cosmology of the earlier religion, Bon Chos, but absorbed its gods, demons and its rituals. Perhaps these are the inspiration for the *Dharmapalas*, the fierce-looking guardians of the law, who feature in the *gompa* dance-dramas.

The theological shift from Hinayana's ascetic mould to the more practical Mahayana ideal of the Bodhisattva removed for Nirvana-seekers the necessity of giving up their worldly concerns. The Mahayana ideal explains the attitude of the lay Buddhist who holds back his own salvation to help others reach the right path. As a consequence, Mahayana Buddhism helped intensify the contact between the monk and the community. In this process, the representational aspect of the Buddha was deified, and a pantheon with personified forms (a departure from earlier practice) was the logical consequence. Under the influence of the Bhakti movement, Buddhist practice underwent major changes. The oral tradition came to be systematised into written texts, and the laity to be socially organised into congregations.

As rituals became more elaborate, the Sutras or canonical texts were compiled, and the emphasis in the religious orders shifted from missionary work to academic learning. Since State protection was ensured, the process of building an intellectual foundation was begun through the efforts of Ring-chen-zang-po when links with India were renewed. Ring-chen-zang-po's translation of Indian texts gave rise to several sects among the Tibetan Buddhists.

Ideas and icons

The deification of the Buddha developed a complex and fascinating iconography. The basic idea is that of the five *Dhyani* Buddhas and their related Bodhisattvas, which are elaborated in the mandalas. The Tantric additions of the female deities are not fully evolved in the older temples or *gompas*.

The *gompa* is the living vehicle of Ladakhi Buddhism and iconography. The entrance of the *du-khang* or the main temple is guarded by the Lords of the Four Quarters. They can be identified by their colours and attributes: North: Kuvera — yellow banner and mongoose; South: Vimdhaka — green or blue, elephant head and sword; East: Dhritarashtra — white, playing the lute; West: Virupaksha — red, carrying a *chorten.*

The sidewall of a gallery also has the Wheel of Life represented by three concentric circles. The innermost signifies anger, desire and ignorance, represented by the cock, the serpent, and the pig, respectively. The middle circle represents the six states of existence — the worlds of the gods and demigods, death, hell, animals and men. The outer circle represents the chain of causation through 12 symbols.

Popularly, the Buddha is represented as Avalokiteswara (the Compassionate One), endowed with 11 heads and a thousand arms; Manjusri (the Wise One) sitting in the lotus posture with a sword and a book; and Maitreya (the Buddha-to-come), depicted standing or enthroned. In all representations, we see the Precious Adornments: Earrings, chains at the neck, chest and waist; bracelets on the wrist and upper arms — signifying the virtues of generosity, patience, energy, meditation, wisdom and self-discipline.

Importance is also attached to the *Dharmapalas:* Mahakala (time), Yamantaka (death), Shugdan and Vajra Bhairava. These are usually to be found in the *la-khang* or the *go-khang*, both inner sanctuaries where women were forbidden access. The female deities are represented as Green and White Taras on either side of the Amitabha figure. They appear on the ceiling of the Kaikani *chorten*. The Dolma Dolkar and the Dolma — Tara images — are often found in the *du-khang*. Sometimes a special temple is dedicated exclusively to the Taras, like the shrine of Tara Doljan at Spituk, where on days ordained by the Tibetan calendar, glass bangles are offered as part of a fertility rite.

Living at close quarters with the supernatural, in a cosmology populated with a host of gods, demons and spirits,

Inside a monastery, Lamas sit in a row and chant from the Kham-jur as one of them strikes the drum and another beats the cymbals

Clockwise: The *dharmachakra* or teaching Buddha at Thikse; Monks in training recite their lessons; The meditating Buddha overlooks the rows of monks at Hemis

Gompas: Breathing Buddhism

The central role of the *Gompa* was based on the political and military role it had played in the early period. The civil and administrative functions were built on land ownership and supplemented by money lending, trade and mortgages. Most *gompas* found in Zanskar, an area known for its religious orientation, belong to the period dating from AD 1400. Here, two sects control the *gompas*, the Drug-pa and the Gelugs-pa.

Gompas have lines of *chorten*, symbolic structures that often house relics. A good example is the one at Karsha, which has the mummified body of an incarnate monk inside it. The oldest *gompa* is at Tandi on the route to Zanskar. Called the Guru Ghantal *gompa*, it had a slanting timber roof which has been replaced with a slate roof. Another old structure, the Sani *Gompa*, is very similar in size and construction. Its Kanika *chorten*, which is said to represent the Kushan emperor Kanishka, is one of the claims of its antiquity.

One of the largest *gompas*, the Karsha *gompa*, is said to have been founded by Padmasambhava. It has an Avalokiteswara temple with wall paintings that recall the Rinchen-tsang-po period.

The great Phugtal *gompa* lies off the gorge of the Tsarap river. Its main temples have been built in a cave in the cliff-face above the river. Wooden ladders and platforms lead to the monks' quarters, which seem to hang in the air. Some of its wall paintings are similar to the Alchi *gompa* in Central Ladakh. The common theme in the *gompa* wall paintings is of incarnating Bodhisattvas come to relieve humanity of its suffering.

The Spituk *gompa* is one of the earliest ones which retains the nucleus of the earlier discussion halls that later expanded into *gompas*

Green (Shyama Tara) Tara is one of the two supreme goddesses of Buddhism, the other being Prajnaparamita. Tara was born from the tears of Avalokiteswara

Ladakhis continue to believe in the efficacy of ancient secret rites of propitiation. Ladakhi folklore warns against the 24 dangers by which a hundred thousand spirits endanger life. Nooks, crannies and rocks painted in mineral tones to ward off the evil eye are visible everywhere. For the same purpose, skulls of dogs and sheep, ibex horns and spears and, of course, prayer flags, dot the countryside around every settlement. This animistic belief in totems and taboos, cutting across ethnic and religious divides, evolved from the Bon Chos rituals of local tribes. As in many societies, which have developed in relative isolation, there is no apparent conflict between civilised religion and the continuing beliefs of more primitive times, permitting co-existence. This is true of their broader vision of life itself. Take for instance modern medicine. Though it was brought by Christian missionaries and is now available throughout the region via the large-scale presence of the Army, a number of Ladakhis still prefer the indigenous system practised by the *Amchis* and the Lha.

The drama of healing

The *Amchis* practice a baffling mixture of science and mysticism known as *swarza* or Science of Life. It is said to have originated at the time of the battle between good and evil in which some gods were injured. To heal them, the Buddha is said to have elaborated the Ayurvedic system. *Gompa* libraries are stocked with the *Samans-Chak text* that has around 600 remedies based on mineral, herbal and animal products.

The special healing abilities of the *Lha* are altogether more spectacular. The present-day Lhas are living oracles of the Spirit of Mercy, the Pal-den Lha-mo, depicted riding a white horse in several *thangkas*. Their occult powers are acquired through several years of rigorous training, the observance of fasts, punishing abstinence and exacting physical control. Knowledge and identification of the causes of both pain and pleasure and their location in the body are essential features of training, together with the learning of proper mantras.

Though held in awe and greatly sought after, the Lha-mos (female) and the Lha-bas (male) have no particular hereditary or other claims to their skill. They are perfectly ordinary people of common occupations who, through their apparent spiritual abilities, achieve status and local fame.

At a fixed time of the morning, the sick, together with their ailing pets, crowd the Lha-mo's house. Incredulous tourists and onlookers swell the crowd as the Lha-mo goes into a trance and begins intoning. An interpreter or medium communicates the Lha-mo's vision to the crowd. The Lha-mo selects patients apparently arbitrarily, while the medium fixes the 'fee' for the cure in terms of *chang* or, now more often, money. It is part of the medium's responsibility to translate this to the patients.

As each patient is called, the Lha-mo sets to work, sometimes with prolonged and vigorous sucking, extracting such strange yet familiar articles as beads, clumps of hair, wads of paper, phlegm and coloured fluid from the patient's body. These pain-causing objects are said to be deposited by the evil eye and as each is extracted, the patient visibly relaxes. Often the treatment has to be repeated and the patient returns on subsequent days with only the memory of the sensation of the Lha-mo's puckered lips against his skin.

Recognising the limitations of her skills, the Lha-mo at times refuses to treat certain maladies, preferring to refer the patient to another Lha-mo or Lha-ba, or even a medical practitioner. However, while in a trance, the Lhas are said to have a certain prescience by which they can also uncover obsessions and psychological fears, and even identify thieves and criminals.

The Lha-bas – male healers – are far more dramatic. After drinking vast quantities of *chang*, they go on a rampage and run the blade of a sharpened sword against their tongues, drawing blood. In this way, it is said, they expel the influence of the evil eye. The sight of a possessed Lha-ba incanting incomprehensible mantras and, in the case of the Lha-mo of Sabu, wielding a sharp whip, can make even the most stout-hearted quail. The medium explains to the hushed and awed spectators the Lha-ba's changing moods, from time to time, appeasing him with draughts of *chang*. As the rage abates and self-control is regained, the healing begins. There is at all times, a shared sense of stupefied horror but while modern Ladakhis and educated tourists are often sceptical, the simple peasant gets a dual benefit. He is not only convinced of his cure but is comforted that the Lha's treatment has given his illness a sanction in the eyes of society. Superstition elaborated by Tantric prescriptions have developed into the equivalent of *shastras* or rules which govern every facet of life. Whether it is dance, arts, crafts, iconography or even architecture, their influence has given an enduring continuity to these traditions.

Bhaisajyaguru is the main Medicine Buddha among a total of eight. His body is blue which is the healing colour; he holds a bowl of nectar in his left hand and a branch of the myrobalan plant in his right hand.

5
Of Space and Structure

The use of space in Ladakh is ordered by the continuity of time and the interconnections that exist between mountain and valley, water and the produce of the land. It seems as if the heart of the earth beats with the same pulse as man's. A similar integration animates local architecture and construction. The construction materials are stone and hand-made, sun-dried bricks with dried mud as plaster. Poplar beams hold up flat roofs compacted from willow branches and earth. *Gompas* and palaces, standing for hundreds of years, have been built with the same simple construction material and techniques.

Over the years, two categories of dwelling have developed – the *avasa* in the rural setting and the *arama* in the urban sites. Boundary walls enclosed both individual and collective dwellings but the *avasa* was a temporary structure on land donated by a patron to mendicant scholars. But, the *arama* turned permanent. The patron supplied the means for the material well-being of the scholar, who reciprocated by initiating and including the patron in learned discussion.

As the membership of these discussions widened, a hall was added. From this kernel, the settlement or dwelling developed into a complex. As the wealthy merchants began to turn increasingly to Buddhism, the *gompa* took shape. Some of the older monasteries like Spituk, Lamayuru and Hemis retain the original nucleus that has been expanded into the present complex. Typically, five significant structures are found in a *gompa*: the *guha* (sanctum), *hanumiya* (administrative block with three floors), *pasada* (residential block with two floors), *addhayoga* (house with curled eaves) and finally the *vihara* (communal dwelling).

A statue of the Buddha at Alchi straddles photographs of the Dalai Lama, the religious head of the Buddhists, who is a much revered figure in Ladakh

As Buddhism changed under Mauryan emperor Ashoka's missionary impetus into an expansionist religion, certain basic tenets of architecture were set. By Kanishka's time, when the schism between Mahayana and Hinayana was complete, the theoretical shift had extended to art. The emphasis within the *gompa* now shifted from missionary work to scholarship and religion became contemplative. The learned texts, the *Tanjur* (3461 texts) and the *Kanjur* (1108 texts), preserve such experiences. The viharas grew into *mahaviharas* and the settlements' size increased with rich murals and carvings. Persecuted monks under pressure from warring principalities found a haven there. When Ladakh faced its expansionist neighbours, the Buddhist system of inter-dependence based on community ties mobilised an impregnable social force to strengthen the already strategically located natural barriers.

Ladakhi architecture was influenced by the ideas brought in by Padmasambhava from Swat and by Atisa from Vikramasila. On the other hand, the Alchi frescoes have a definite Mughal character, introduced by the Tibetan scholar Rin-chen-zang-po. He had been ordered by King Yesh-es-od to Kashmir and other Buddhist centres of North India to assimilate local traditions, which were then transported to Guje.

The prototype of the *gompa* was the monastery at Sam-ya in Tibet, with its mandala symmetry, in a plan oriented towards the cardinal points. The central temple was three-tiered, and the enclosing walls interrupted with *chortens* or wall paintings showing the Wheel of Life and colossal figures and demons, all of which figure in later monasteries. As classical civilisation in India evolved into medieval civilisation, a new art style was introduced into Kashmir. This was absorbed in Ladakh.

All the major monasteries of Ladakh stand on rocky summits with a typical hierarchy of buildings. As soon as you step inside one, you realise the importance of the small window openings, the only source of illumination other than the butter lamp, often substituted by a kerosene lantern and now by electricity. Standing in the dark room, surrounded by an eerie silence that incorporates centuries of experience and religious absorption, the visitor is struck by the ambience of Ladakh, generally explained away as the 'spirit of Buddhism'.

In this trans-Himalayan rain shadow zone, where a small community supports itself at a low level of technology and under severe environmental constraints, there is bound to be

a strong link between the socio-economic and religious aspects of life. The monastery's share-cropping role which brought in so much wealth that the surplus was converted into gold, silver and art treasures, made it the natural victim of siege and attack on flat ground. So it was that the *gompa* was moved to a hilltop where the monastery and tile fortress combined into a single defence unit.

In Spituk, we can no longer see the symmetrical arrangement so visible at Thikse and Hemis. The emerging style of architecture formed certain characteristics: white sloping small windows, balconies at every level and a rising hierarchy of buildings, the temple decorated with umbrellas and flags at the highest level, and a medley of residential and administrative buildings at the base. The courtyard is approached by an entrance where Cham dances and communal activities can be accommodated. A circumambulatory passage surrounds the temple with a row of prayer wheels that are rotated once, three times, or a hundred and eight times. The main portico generally has the Wheel of Life and the Dharmapato, before passing to the chapel, the *du-khang* (assembly room) and the *lha-khang* (sanctum). Beyond these lies the *zimchung*, the

A mandala wall mural at Alchi is supposed to aid contemplation and meditation personal room of the *kushok* or head priest. The *gon-khang* is the chapel of the guardian deities and holds the weapons and the masks. Then there are the cloisters and other utilities.

Special mention must be made of the *chortens* though they are not strictly a part of the monastery but are located in its vicinity. Inspired by the Indian stupa, the *chorten* was already a cult symbol. In recent excavations, a timber column has been found at the centre of the stupa. This implies that it was more than just a house for relics: It was the symbolic representation of the Tree of Life. Once this cult association developed, the stupa underwent certain changes so that it could be miniaturised and made portable for the faithful.

In this alteration, regional attributes changed the appearance of the *chorten*. The semi-spherical shape changed into clusters of umbrellas, placed one over the other in 13 tiers. There are eight types of *chortens*. They relate to eight events in the Buddha's life, the eight cardinal points, eight original stupas in India and the eight manifestations. Their sizes vary and the materials can be stone, mud, brick or plaster, timber, silver, gold or brass.

Chortens are found close to every settlement. The bell-like portions hold the mortal remains and belongings of revered monks who have spent their lives in giving spiritual support to the community. The Namgyal *chorten* invokes the Goddess Namgyal, the Sku-dug *chorten* invokes the Buddha, and the Ring-sel, which is considered the most important, represents the jewels in the heart of the Buddha, synonymous with peace for the sangha. *Chortens* also form part of the complex system of symbols that ward off the evil eye. The Tisseru, one of the oldest *chortens* on the outskirts of Leh, encloses a mule-shaped rock believed to be the most evil of all natural phenomena. Pointed peaks overlooking a range that protects settlements are also considered indications of the evil eye, and are associated with bad weather. To counter this, *chortens* are built facing these peaks.

Linking *chortens*, stretching far and wide across the land, are *mane* walls. The name is derived from the mantra, *Om Mane Padme Hum*, inscribed on every stone and rock that makes up the structure. The *mane* wall also serves a practical purpose and has now become a symbol of Buddhism in Ladakh. Each of the *mane* stones is a devotee's offering of thanksgiving. Beginning as a small square or round edifice, it grows into a wall about four metres wide. The Red sect keeps the wall to

the left while the Yellow sect keeps it to the right. Result: The wall is often located in the centre of a path. Nimmo, Stok and Hemis along with Leh provide a view of some of the oldest *mane* walls. To the Buddhist, the *mane* wall is a necklace, each stone a jewel expressing the joy of thanksgiving over several years. These days, professional *mane* stone-makers fashion individual stones for the tourist.

At some time, sighting a *mane* wall or *chorten* must have caused a lightening of the pilgrim's and the merchant's load, indicating the possibility of refreshment in the precincts of a nearby monastery. Today, it is a symbol of what the tourist is about to see, a precious sentinel on the path to rediscovering one's spirit.

Facing page:
Ibex horns, mane wall stones and *chortens* are considered to bring good fortune
Below: The secular and the religious intertwine at Thikse

Preceding pages 58-59: Novices find monastic childhood a light affair in the Lamasery
Below: Cham dancers engage in a mock battle in the morality tradition of Ladakh

6

Cultures in a Crucible

When one talks of Ladakh's culture, it is the West Tibetan influence – dominant up to the late medieval period – that comes immediately to mind, after which we see the influx of Islamic and Hindu traditions. Ladakh is divided into clearly defined cultural zones. West of Mulbekh lies the Islamic centre of Kargil. It incorporates many aspects of the lifestyle of the Kashmir valley and some of the Indus valley; east of Mulbekh is the Buddhist citadel, Leh, with its treasured monasteries and murals, vast altars and gilded icons, brocaded fabrics, illuminated manuscripts and masterpieces in metal-work.

Ladakhi crafts reflect the splendour of nature's tints, using rust-red, ochre and umber from the fossil-rich rocks, amethyst, lapis and turquoise to embellish these tones, and the gold of the sunrise or the smoky purple of twilight to reflect the life-giving forces. Spinning and weaving of wool, metal work, wood carving and *thangka* paintings have been the favoured crafts. But Ladakhis seem to prefer dance, music and literature to the patient and dedicated commitment demanded by crafts. The arts of Ladakh are closely related to Buddhism and its precursor Bon Chos. This is the sacred backdrop to what we now consider a secular tradition.

Music and dance

Ladakh's religious dance remains within the Tibetan tradition whereas the social dances, *Pome-chas,* danced by women, and *Pu-che-chas,* danced by men, are being developed for the stage. But they are seen best in their natural setting at a village wedding or an archery contest. Buddhist society, though open

'Skeletons' clown
among the audience
at the Cham dance,
a regular feature of
gompa festivals

and free, does not have a strong formal educational system, because the monastic tradition dominates. Dance has traditionally filled this hiatus, offering an informal avenue for teaching social norms.

Music in the mountains arises from nature like a plaintive sigh; it's not the structured achievement of a formal system evolved by societies with a long urban history. No social event or activity – sowing or harvesting, a wedding or a festival – is complete without music. In the past, music was not a form of entertainment; it was either part of a religious ceremony or related to the life of the people. But musicians who earlier had easy access to local patronage, are entertainers today, having joined the stream of migrants to the township after the closure of the old trade routes interrupted the dispersal of goods and services.

The most vital Ladakhi musical form is *Lha-ringa*, which consists of 360 tunes. It is only played at Shey for the dance of the oracle at the time of the pre-harvest celebrations. Parts of the *Lha-ringa* are played at all auspicious occasions, particularly when there is a ceremonial feast for incarnate lamas. Specific ceremonial music is connected with the arrival and departure of dignitaries. Exorcists use it to overpower evil spirits and sports-lovers to express their appreciation.

Earlier, when the Namgyal kings were more than just Jagirdars of Stok, concerts were held on the roof of Leh Palace at Lo-sar (New Year) and Dos-mo-che (the winter festival). Noble ladies danced the *Khatuk-chermo* celebrating the glory of Ladakh and the dynasty. The *Khan-mon,* the royal musicians, played the music. Although the *Khatuk-chermo* festival has now been altered to cater to the modern tourist, it is only a shadow of the rich tradition of Ladakh's popular culture.

Just as the cycle of festival songs is evidence of Ladakh's oral poetic tradition, the Kesar Saga is the national epic, a collection of songs and proverbs. It's also an anthology of myths surrounding the story of creation and the development of a civilisation based on the valour and genius of 18 heroes. Tales of Kesar, the king of the land called Ling, and his exploits in subduing evil giants, have much in common with Indian myths. Along with Cho-cho-dogur-ma, the heroine, he participates in many adventures, now serialised on radio.

The literary style of Ladakh owes much to the rhythm of the music. Most verse begins with an invocation to the sun, the very giver of life in such desolate emptiness. There are good

Travelling Thangkas

Rare and beautiful *thangkas* from the Lamaseries of Ladakh are being sent around the country at the initiative of the Central Institute of Buddhist Studies, Leh. The exhibition will end up at the Institute of Higher Tibetan Studies in Sarnath. The exhibit has benefited the paintings as they have been restored. Yet, some *thangkas* are more than 300 years old and their colours are fading and the paint is cracking.

Thangkas narrate incidents from the life of the Buddha, the Bodhisattavas or illustrate the Sakyamuni's teachings and sermons. Earlier, only experts appreciated this art. But, their visual appeal has attracted the layperson and many countries in the Himalaya are using *thangkas* as souvenirs. These silken masterpieces attract the attention of the faithful because they are rich with meaning. The use of natural colours made from stone ensures that the colour lasts. The *thangka* is a religious object which has a strict code of representation and needs consecration by lamas to infuse it with a divine spirit.

luck symbols too, like the numeral three. There are regional forms like the *zha-bra* of Chang Thang and, due to the Balti influence, the *ghazal.* The most endearing are what may be termed patriotic songs and those that extol the virtues of the home village. The state is now compiling a repertoire of folk verse. A similar tradition underlies nuptial songs.

The 'work' songs which accompany every phase of the agricultural cycle are equally varied: Harvesting songs rise in a chorus over the golden fields when the sickle flashes like lightning. Winnowing songs are whimsical solos sung to lighten the tedium of separating the chaff. Ploughing is accompanied by robust songs in praise of fertility, the gift of gods who chastise the earth into bearing fruitful seed. Women working on irrigation channels sing in tune to the melting music of mountain cascades. From Ladakh's ancient past we have Dardic culture which is unique to Chingtan. In contrast with rigorous practitioners of Islam, the Dards who were not overly intimidated by the stern Aghas of Kargil, have absorbed Buddhist ways. The Bropkas (Buddhist Dards) have retained their 'racial purity' and customs by maintaining strict insularity. Yet, their village festivities, the *Bono-na,* are similar to those in the rest of the district. It is illustrative of their composite culture that the Chingtan *gompa* is looked after by a Muslim.

The Ladakhis find it difficult to articulate and define their folk culture. Since it is so much a part of their daily life, they have not tried to seek its sources, study it or record its historical development. Some visitors will catch its spirit and identify with its rhythm, others will walk away with an impression of Ladakh's physical beauty, remaining unaware of its cultural wealth.

Winter in Ladakh is a period of inactivity and rest. Earlier, the poorer Ladakhis used to migrate to Kashmir for work, but now government work has extended the earning period. Most people can take time off for the *gompa* festival, solemn and dignified till the ceremonies, but later becoming a *tamasha.*

Festival ceremonies begin with the unfurling of the *thangka.* The *rinpoche* or head lama enters and is ceremonially seated. The lamas are summoned by the drums. Each enters with his hands raised above his head, then prostrates himself before the sanctified disciples of the Sakyamuni. Recitations from the sacred texts are followed by instrumental music, which includes drums, horns, cymbals and bells. The hautboys, made of wood with silver mouthpieces, and eight to 10-feet long

copper trumpets, are the central part of the procession. Recitation, chants and music alternate with Cham dances. A motley crowd packs the rafters. What appears esoteric to the non-Buddhist audience captivates the Buddhist spectators who sit in rapt attention through the sombre spectacle.

The papier mâché masks represent ferocious beings, *Mahakalis* and *Dakinis,* and the symbolic movement of the dancers is related to exorcising evil spirits. Each gesture in the slow and measured dance is meaningful. The lay audience identifies the character by the mask, the colour of the costume

Top: Cultural events at the Sindhu Darshan festival
Facing page: Beads and necklaces add colour to the Ladakhi woman's dress
Pages 66-67: Scene of a wedding at Stok

65

and the handkerchief. Often, the head of the family stands in the midst of the dancers, fulfilling a vow or making an offering to the *gompa*. Outside, tea *chang* (a barley wine) and a ceremonial meal are made ready. The bazaar is set up and gossip and business carry on side by side. No event is restricted to a single household; families extend over villages; and the stranger is welcomed with a shy smile.

Rites of passage

Marriages are occasions for revelry and everyone participates with gaiety. A Ladakhi marriage is generally initiated by the groom's family with an offering of *chang* to the bride's family. Often the go-between is the lama. If the match is accepted, the lama is consulted and the date fixed. Although in towns, the families share the cost incurred, the community bears most of the expenditure of the marriage feast. Each family contributes something: wheat, barley, sugar, apricots, butter or milk. An account is kept of the gift that has to be returned in equal measure during a similar event in the guest's family. *Kha-taks*, ceremonial scarves, are offered to the bridal couple. The bride sits demurely through the rites; the groom joins in the merriment.

Muslim weddings are similar except for the segregation of male and female guests and drinking of tea instead of *chang*. Often the groom returns to the bride's house if her family does not have a son. Divorced individuals and poorer families have the sanction to celebrate a marriage 'by theft', where the bride is brought home quietly and only relatives and close friends are invited to a meal after a few days.

The birth of a child is also an occasion for the community to come close. Friends and relatives visit with special food for the mother and the lamas are called to pray for the health of the newborn. Earlier, the infant was taken to the blacksmith's shop to inhale odours which keep away evil spirits. When a grandson is old enough to work in the field, the grandparents may sometimes move to a cottage and cultivate a small plot to make way for the new generation. The joint family is still the norm in Ladakh with the elder son assuming a patriarchal role and caring for the family's well being. Often the eldest daughter of a Buddhist family that has no sons takes on the same role.

Centres of craft

The Ladakhi crafts tradition had a narrow base as it was confined to the needs of a self-sufficient agrarian economy, dependent on its own pool of artisans. Essential goods such as grain and raw wool were traditionally exchanged for salt and tea, while luxury items came through the Leh trading centre. Much of Ladakh's culture even today reflects the need to keep the *'kafila'* – life-line – going. With the intervention of the cash economy, this village-based tradition was not strong enough to extend its skills. Today, mass-produced goods dominate the local markets.

In Chiling, the centre for metal workers, families make tea-urns, mostly of copper or brass. Gold ornaments that were the specialty of four Nepalese families are rare today, but silver work has survived. The best of this craft can be seen in the *gompa* treasures or in the homes of rich Ladakhis who have inherited jewellery and ceremonial dishes from their mother. For most, seeing a Ladakhi woman in festival finery is often the only way of glimpsing some rare silver ornaments today.

Decorative *gur-gur* tea churns, and the *chogtse*, a typical Ladakhi table, low and ornamented, can be found at the crafts centre at Leh. But these are no longer as fine as those of old, when the craftsman was an artisan and not a souvenir producer. Ladakh did not need to develop a craft culture by virtue of its location on the Silk Route. Every luxury item was brought from somewhere else so that though every village had a weaver, an artisan and a blacksmith, they didn't necessarily refine their skills. But, with the curtailment of trade with Sinking and the closure of the Chang Thang trail, Ladakh has begun to develop a carpet-weaving industry using Tibetan motifs. This craft is still in its infancy. Pashmina is also woven as a result of the handicraft fever that has gripped India, but there is no effort to capture the cashmere's smoothness; rather, the emphasis is on the natural and hardy look.

Winter is the time to work the loom or to weave a carpet. As the weaver's spindle turns, and the hands fly over the emerging pattern of the Tibetan dragon in search of eternal peace, the sunlight becomes warmer and the sky less magnificently blue; the bones seem to rest easier and

the sinews quicken with the desire to break free of the constraint of winter's labour. Summer, short but sweet, beckons with its own demands.

At the crossing of the pilgrim and shepherd routes there is plenty of life — thousands of sheep, pashmina goats and yaks tended by shepherds who have perhaps never heard of Delhi. Many names they are familiar with are not on the trekking map, and marked by nothing other than a heap of flat stones or a tattered prayer flag. At the high-altitude pastures of Chang Thang, shepherds pitch their goatskin tents, like so many black umbrellas, around which the herds graze peacefully in summer. These high-altitude meadows are the home of the *kiang*, the wild ass, glimpsed so indistinctly by the traveller. Its reddish brown body and flying black mane are the only spots of colour against the still, silent world of bleak, bare rock. The herd thunders past and a single horse stops to paw the earth. Suddenly it tosses its head, gazes around, neighs shrilly and vanishes. The *kiang* is always in rapid flight.

The nomads are denied the joy of seeing miles of barley waving under sunlit skies. Nor do they share in the pride of husbanding a fine crop. Their existence revolves around the urgency of finding pastures. Their cash flow depends on the pashmina, but their flock includes yaks and the *huniya* sheep. The yak is the mainstay of the nomad's life, providing milk, butter and meat, and material for the tent-like canopies woven from its hair. The sheep is a source of coarse wool. Only when an animal becomes a burden on the shepherd's scarce resources, is it slaughtered. Culling from the flock occurs only at the start of winter, a schedule that is evidence of unerring Ladakhi logic: Conserving scarce fodder and at the same time using winter's natural refrigeration.

Most people find *chang* more appetising than *gur-gur*, the buttered tea which tastes like weak broth, or *sheer-chai*, the salted tea with its lurid pink colour and acquired taste. Everyone takes a few turns at the tea-urn that churns out the buttered tea, drunk copiously in the dry climate. The wood stove that burns day and night in the kitchen reflects both time past and present. For the outsider, the landscape of Ladakh is so imposing, the air so pure, nothing seems to be as we have earlier known or perceived it. To be present when dawn awakens the rising mountain from the mist is the moment when we acknowledge that, and submit to the indomitability of nature. The mind is free to roam far beyond what the eye can see; to delight in the spread of nature's bounty under a benign sky; to share in the struggle against adversity; to be completely alone in uninhabited space, forcefully aware of individual boundaries, yet finding solace in the community.

As if to contemplate this, modern Ladakhi homes have a *shel-khang* or glass room. It evolved from the *rup-sel*, an open balcony, which when glazed makes passive use of solar energy, creating a hot-house effect, besides keeping the wind out. Usually the glass room is spacious, low ceilinged and with little furniture. The view it offers is its only embellishment — the only one it needs. There is nothing more relaxing than to sit by the window, a part of this grand canvas, the importance of one's existence reduced to its proper scale.

For the young Ladakhis, sleeping under the stars which shine like lanterns in the midnight blue sky, summer passes like a dream, all too soon. It is a kind season for an ebullient and joyous people who always find something to smile at. Particularly when the sun is bright and the *scurin-ba* festivities get under way, *chang* vessels are brought out from the cellar and briskly consumed by the all-male crowd. There is an abundance of smoke, noise and good-humoured clowning. As the drums begin, there is dancing. The feet move in a slow and shuffling motion, but the arms wave in all directions, the hands holding a white *khat-tak*, a loosely woven scarf, in lieu of a garland of flowers. In the afternoon, everyone returns home to change into ceremonial dress and the men to collect bows and arrows for the archery contest.

The menu is an eloquent reminder of the gastronomic and cultural streams that make up Ladakh. The diet is poor in variety and quality because it's dependent on the seasons and the scarce availability of ingredients. But it is well suited to the climate for each dish contains ingredients vital to compensate for the dryness and cold. *Tsampa* (parched barley flour mixed into a gruel) is eaten with buttered tea or *chang* to combat the rigours of the climate. Well-to-do Ladakhis vary their diet with *thug-kpas* (soup of meat, vegetables and small flat noodles), or *pa-ba* (mixed flour of roasted 'naked' barley and *kerzey* gram) added to soup, *chang* or tea. Another popular dish is *sky* — fried wheat-flour dumplings mixed with meat, potatoes and turnips. Most dishes are steamed, although today the richer households will add *tarka* (seasoned butter or oil) to a dish. Most visitors relish *mok-mok*, steam-cooked meat dumplings or *gya-tuk*, Chinese-style egg noodles.

Games people play

Polo is an integral part of summer activities, played anywhere and with any number of players, depending on the size of the level ground and the number of skilled players available. It has always been a popular Central Asian sport, although today it is chiefly associated with the British. What one sees in Ladakh is the Balti style of polo, where the player is allowed to handle the ball and throw it into the goal. The chukkas of the games are divided into nine goals and the only foul is to cut across the path of another horseman. Skill is defined by a flamboyant style of horsemanship and a steady eye. The Baltis from Chushot are still the best players, and popular opinion ascribes the introduction of polo to Ladakh through the Balti mother of Sengge Namgyal. Other than Leh, Chushot is the only village of central Ladakh that has its own polo ground.

In contrast, archery contests follow a strict etiquette. The team captains must belong to the best families and preferably should be their senior members. Music accompanies the shooting, and a round of *chang* celebrates a bull's-eye. In Kargil, where Islamic tradition frowns on levity, the standard of archery is much higher, while in the Buddhist areas, the gala spirit is keener. Villagers assemble in a smoothed-out hollow where the target is set. After the contest, the crowd shifts to a sheltered spot for dancing and more *chang* drinking. The honour of leading the dance goes to the winner. While the men swagger and stamp their feet, the women join hands and with much vivacity move in a circle in regular step, often singing as they dance. The winner, somewhat unfairly, has to host a feast for the losers, so quite often he disclaims the honour and the result is in dispute. Sometimes it even ends up in the law courts. At dinner, sheep are slaughtered and a lot of time is spent eating.

Ladakhi *tagi* or bread is a delicious accompaniment to soup, or with butter and *lassi* (buttermilk) or *dahi* (curd) often seasoned with herbs. *Choo-tagi* is easy to digest and similar in taste to flour dumplings; *shab-motagi* is made from wheat flour, much like the Mughal *rumali roti,* and *kham-bir tagi* is made from flour which is slightly fermented before cooking. *Thal-tag tagi* is about two cm in diameter, and cooked like a Spanish omelette. *Kho-tak* is both a sweet and savoury *sattu halwa,* similar to *pa-ba.* Children like having it with sugar and butter; adults with salted tea.

March of modernism

Since 1962, when the borders between China, India and Pakistan were sealed and the importance of trade was undermined, Ladakh's culture has transformed with a new value being attached today to land and livestock. Daily life has been eroded by forces outside people's perceptions. The cultural impact has been so subtle and yet so pervasive that one may fail to notice the wedge driven into the historical alignments.

Many have cast their covetous eyes on Ladakh, a kingdom of peace and serenity. They have hoped to subdue the heart of Central Asia. Today, three hostile neighbours are attempting to redefine a historical unity in the name of narrow nationalism. This goes against the balance of cultural inter-dependence of the trans-Himalayan ranges. Here the exchange of goods, tolerance between faiths and respect for boundaries have given the Ladakhi a broad-mindedness that must not be destroyed.

The recent inclusion of Ladakh into Jammu and Kashmir has to recognise that alien symbols have been welded together which cannot be wished away from the Ladakhi identity. Also, the aspiration of the people to conserve and protect a special historical experience even as they become part of the mainstream has to be taken count of. As the Buddhists say: 'We reveal to the mind of him who asks, that which is understood by him.'

Ladakh is once more at the crossroads. There is the crisis of the break with Tibetan scholasticism, the closing down of the Yarkand trail and the disappearance of the old Silk Route. In its place, we have the spirit of modernisation that once again challenges its old adversaries—nature, history and reality.

Preceding pages 68-69:
Ladakhis have the most
vivid variety of headgear
Top: Balti ponies make for
speed and enthusiasm
during Ladakh's
polo matches

Preceding pages 72-73: The polo ground at Leh town
Below: Zanskar, where hospitable fields and sunburnt faces greet you

7
Manali-Zanskar-Leh

Zanskar is a cul-de-sac formed by the axis of several mountain ranges as they spread from east to west. The panoramic sweep of the valley is replaced with a closed-in mountain trap. The ancient sea floor, strewn with rock falls is no longer benign. There is stillness, everything seems to hang precariously, to be awaiting a thunderclap or a heaving of the already high and desolate mountains to even greater heights.

To the north, we have the Karakoram and to the south, the Great Himalaya range. Between them rise the Ladakh and Zanskar mountain ranges. They can be reached from Kashmir via Kishtwar, from Baltistan in the north, from the south via Kullu and Lahul, and from the east through Chang-Thang. None of these routes is easy and all of them operate for just four or five months of the year. It is surprising therefore that the Zanskar valley has played such a pivotal role in the trade network that was so essential for the survival of the communities that inhabited the closed valleys of Ladakh. Moreover, it was not the Shamma of the Leh bazaar that traded with Zanskar but the Chang-pas of Rupshu who depended on this region for their food supply and other requirements.

Rangdum is the entry into the Zanskar valley. Physically a part of the Suru valley, Rangdum is socially and culturally integrated with Zanskar. Although the valley is predominantly Muslim, this village seems to be a Buddhist outpost. It is here trekkers can hire horses, which continue to be the main transport. Trekkers are drawn by the *gompas* at Sani, Karsha, Stongde and Phugtal. This is also the home of the brown bear, which feeds on nature's bounty and is rarely seen plundering the farms for food.

The new trail: from Leh to Manali

If one had the courage, winter trekking would be easier as the streams would freeze, but the temperatures would fall below −30 degrees Celsius. The favoured season is from July to September and it is possible now to take the road from Manali across the Rohtang pass and Baralacha-la to Padam. But, this journey requires fitness and gear to get you across high passes. A two-day trip takes you to Leh from Manali, something unimaginable two decades ago. The Army presence and tourism have transformed access to Ladakh and the Zanskar valley is no longer closed, although still forbidding.

The Manali route crosses four passes and is open for three to four months. There is hardly any habitation over more than half the route. A journey along this route involves planning for self-sufficiency, since the road is lonely and camps for night halts provide minimal services. There are no gas stations or mechanics, so travelling in convoys is encouraged. A four-wheel drive is essential since rock falls are common. The 200-km journey at heights of over 4,000 metres is not suited for everyone, although it does help acclimatisation.

As one takes the road out of Manali towards the Rohtang Pass, the Beas River flows alongside. Orchards line up the route to Palchan from where the hairpin bends take the heights of the Pir Panjal range, an offshoot of the Greater Himalaya. As one nears Rohtang, a spring wells up. This is the source of the Beas that gives Manali its special charm. Although not as impressive as its approach, the pass at 3,978 metres is broad and open. The hot tea and *pakoras* are enticing after the climb. Weather changes are sudden and blizzards can arrive in no time. Rohtang watchers in the bazaar will tell you whether you can make it across in time or not.

Lahul: hot potatoes

We now enter Lahul, not considered a part of the trans-Himalaya since the Greater Himalaya lies ahead. The common feature is that both regions are in the rain shadow zone. The Chandra and the Bhaga river valleys constitute Upper Lahul. The rivers meet at Kyelang, the district capital. The Kullu architecture is replaced with flat roofs, small windows, adobe and brick structures, which can survive the heavy snows. Deep

gorges, lofty mountains and dark gullies said to form the route for Lord Shiva's *baraat* (wedding party), from Kinnaur Kailash to the home of Goddess Parvati, are the gateway to the valley. Green potato fields, vines of hops and peas and the ochre of the riverbank mark Lahul. Women toil endlessly to transform the cold desert into a region of plenty. Men do the marketing of the wealth and Lahul is now the land of potato farmers. Five families control the potato wealth and their scions are found in Manali, promoting adventure tourism. The Lahul Potato Marketing Society is one of the best co-operatives in the state. It runs the petrol pump at Keylang and a hotel in Manali.

Lahulis are proud of their community that includes Dolma Dicky, the youngest woman to ever climb Everest in 1993, and Tashi Angmo, who has won accolades for family welfare.

Top: A panoramic view of Manali
Facing page (bottom): A sign informing travellers of the passes on the Manali-Leh road

77

August is the month of celebration. The dingy wooden structures of Kyelang's bazaar are dressed up. The *chorten* at the bazaar's end is white-washed and the revel continues through the day and night. The early days of the traffic between Ladakh and Tibet have now given way to Gaddi herdsmen on higher pastures. Sheep can hold up convoys and it is a part of the tradition of the area to give way to the herds.

Traversing the old trade routes

Lahul, Kullu and Zanskar became the source region through the yearly markets set up for barter and cash purchase. The supply of salt and the harvest determined the barter rate – five sheep loads of salt for four bushels of barley or wheat. The barter relationship meant the sheep were sheared on the spot, and the traders became 'mitr', in a ceremony that sanctified their relationship. This meant the same traders met year after year, generation after generation. Money transactions carried on between the bigger traders.

Today there are changes. Zanskar is a part of Kargil district and closer to the Suru valley. It is a trough between two rivers, the Stod and the Lungnak that join to form the Zanskar river. The two rivers have their distinctive green and blue and many people stand on the road ledge for the magnificent view. The heavy snowfall in the valley feeds the glaciers.

The size of the flood plain has made Zanskar a grain basket, since the population is small (20,000) and the wasteland is being brought under the plough. The Zanskar people are not motivated to entrepreneurship since their region produces enough to barter. It is also difficult to access: The Pensi-la Pass at 4,400 metres that links the region to Kargil being the only one that has a motorable road. The arrival of the Chang-pa in June and September to trade with the local inhabitants has become a part of the region's life cycle The traders follow two routes into Zanskar. The first via Debring, south of Taglang-la, which keeps with the Leh-Manali trade route and over the Lunga-Lacha-la to Serchu. Turning north over the Chumik-Marpo-la, they reach the Lungnak valley at Tangtse. This is a 14-day trek for each side of the journey. The traders travel in a group up to Padum from where they branch off to the Zanskar villages. Once their stock is bartered they meet at Padum for the return journey.

Top: Inside Lamayuru, the contemplative Buddha
Facing page: One of the Drokpas, a tribe that claims to be of pure Aryan blood

JAMMU AND KASHMIR

The Indus, flowing north-west to south-east, forms the main watershed that links Tibet with the Central Asian plateau to the north. To the south of the watershed are the valleys of the Dras, the Suru, and the Zanskar that flow into the Indus at Dras, Kargil and Nyemo. Above the valleys, rise the great ridges that have opened up the impenetrable barriers of the Ladakh and Zanskar ranges at Zoji-la, Namik-la and Fotu-la. In the far south, over the Thagang-la, the Zanskar cuts a gorge that meets the high ridge of the Lunga Lacha-la and Bara Lacha-la, which formed the traditional route to the hidden valleys of Lahul and Spiti. In the north-east lies the Khardong-la, which opens into the Shyok valley; beyond which the Karakoram pass leads to Yarkand. To the east lie the Aksai Chin and the salt lakes, Pangong Tso and Tso Morari. It is at the crossroads of this north-south axis that the Buddhist citadel of Leh stands.

CHINA

Karakoram Range

K2 (8,611m)
Pioneer Peak
Masherbrum (7,821m)
7,785m
Rakaposhi (7,788m)
Gilgit
Chilas
Indus river
Nanga Parbat (8,125m)
Skardu

Shyok river
Khardung La (5,602m)
Satti
Khardung
Shyok
Chang La (5,599m)
Pangong Lake
Chushul
Mahe
Nyoma
Lake Tso-Morari

Ladakh Range
Indus river
Marol
Kargil
Shergol
Lamayuru
Nimu
Phanjila
Ranbirpura
LEH
Karu
Upshi
Kumdok
Himis Peak
Tanglang La (5,360m)
Pang
Karzok
Indus river

Dras
Matayan
Suru

Zanskar river
Baralacha-La (4,892m)

Zoji-la (3,529m)
Sonamarg
Awantipur
Bijbiara
Anantnag
Gund
Kishtwar
Doda
Bhadarwah
Ramnagar

Wular Lake
Sopur
Baramula
Uri
Punch
SRINAGAR
Jhelum river
Kot Bainka
Rajauri
Naushahra
Riasi
Udhampur

Line of Control
Jhelum river

INDIA

Zanskar Range

Himachal Pradesh
Ravi river
Chenab river
JAMMU

PAKISTAN

MANALI-LEH ROAD ROUTE

LEH
Karu
Upshi
Tanglang La (5,360m)
More Plains
Pang
Lachalang-La 5,060m
Sarchu
Baralacha-La
Sural Tal
4,895m
Chandra
Darcha
KEYLONG
Tandi
Chenab
Rohtang La 3,978m
Palchan
MANALI

51
60
39
26
23
54
32
75
8
55
52

Indus

Distance between two points in km (Total 475 km)
32